Looking at Dolphins and Porpoises

Dorothy Hinshaw Patent

DAN FEICHT, CEDAR POINT, SANDUSKY, OHIO

Holiday House/New York

Every effort was made to find clear photographs with plenty of contrast, but because dolphins and porpoises are difficult to photograph, some of the pictures may seem slightly out of focus.

Copyright © 1989 by Dorothy Hinshaw Patent
All rights reserved
Printed in the United States of America
Designed by Marjorie Zaum
First Edition

Library of Congress Cataloging-in-Publication Data

Patent, Dorothy Hinshaw.
Looking at dolphins and porpoises / Dorthy Hinshaw Patent.—1st ed.
p.   cm.
Includes index
Summary: Discusses the characteristics and habits, the family life
and intelligence of dolphins and porpoises.
ISBN 0-8234-0748-9
1. Dolphins—Juvenile literature. 2. Porpoises—Juvenile
literature. [1. Dolphins. 2. Porpoises.] I. Title.
QL737.C432P384   1989
599.5'3—dc19   88-39985   CIP   AC

ISBN 0-8234-0748-9

Contents

1. FAMILIAR ANIMALS 4

2. LIVING IN WATER 10

3. SOCIAL LIFE 20

4. HAVING A FAMILY 26

5. FEASTING ON FISH 32

6. DOLPHINS AND PEOPLE 37

7. DOLPHIN SHOW-OFFS 39

8. DOLPHIN INTELLIGENCE 43

   Index 48

1
Familiar Animals

Sea Mammals

The sleek bodies and friendly faces of dolphins and porpoises make them popular animals. These graceful swimmers spend all their lives in the water. They may look like fish, but they are mammals. Like humans and other mammals, dolphins and porpoises are warm-blooded. Their body temperature remains warm, even when the water they live in is cold. Fish breathe through their gills, which allow them to get oxygen from the water. But dolphins and porpoises breathe air. Instead of gills, each dolphin or porpoise has a breathing opening, or blowhole, on top of its head. The blowhole leads to the animal's lungs. When the animal is underwater, the blowhole is closed, but when it comes to the surface, the blowhole opens up. Old air is breathed out and new air comes in.

The blowhole of a killer whale. STEPHEN MULLANE

Dolphin, Porpoise, or Whale?

How can you tell a dolphin from a porpoise? This is not an easy question. Some people use different names for the same kind of animal. A few scientists, for example, call the familiar bottle-nosed dolphin the "bottle-nosed porpoise."

But most scientists agree that there are just six kinds of porpoises. Unlike most dolphins, these animals do not have a beak and their teeth look like little shovels. The teeth of dolphins, on the other hand, are shaped like small cones.

Six kinds of dolphins are usually called whales. The killer whale, for example, is actually a giant dolphin. Pilot whales are also big dolphins.

Altogether, there are about forty-five different kinds or species of dolphins and porpoises. Here, the word "dolphins" will be used when general comments are made.

The pilot whale is actually a kind of dolphin.
THOMAS JEFFERSON,
MOSS LANDING
MARINE LABS

A killer whale leaping
from the water, called
"breaching."
JIM HEIMLICH-BORAN/
THE WHALE MUSEUM

How Big Are Dolphins?

Most dolphins are large—from 6 to 9 feet (1.8 to 2.7 meters) long
and weigh between 200 and 400 pounds (90.7 to 181 kilograms).
Even the smallest, called the Fransicana, is more than 4 feet (1.25
meters) long and weighs over 45 pounds (20 kilograms).

The killer whale is the largest dolphin. A full-grown male can
be 31 1/2 feet (9.6 meters) long. That's as long as six adults lying
head-to-foot on the floor. A big killer whale may weigh nine tons
(8,200 kilograms).

Where Dolphins Live

Most dolphins and porpoises live in the sea. They are found in all the world's oceans. Each kind, however, has its own special needs. Some, like the harbor porpoise, usually stay close to land. Others—the hourglass dolphin, for example—live far from land. Killer whales stay in cold water. Other species, like the Hawaiian spinner dolphin, need warm water to survive.

The spinner dolphin is a graceful swimmer.
C. ALLAN MORGAN

An Amazon River dolphin. JEN AND DES BARTLETT/BRUCE COLEMAN INC.

But there are five kinds of dolphins that live in rivers. These river dolphins have their own scientific family. They have very long, thin beaks with many teeth. Their eyes are small and don't see well. There are no river dolphins in North America. They are only found in South America and Asia.

2

Living in Water

Long long ago, the ancestors of dolphins lived on land. These ancient animals had four legs and hairy bodies. But over many many generations, dolphins slowly changed. They became better and better suited to their life in the water.

Their bodies developed a streamlined shape that makes them slip smoothly through the water as they swim. They are no longer covered with hair. A few have some bristles on their heads, and the Amazon River dolphin has some on its beak. That is all that is left of the hair that keeps most mammals warm.

The smooth, slippery skin of the dolphin ripples as it swims, helping it slide quickly through the water. Hair would slow it down. Instead of hair to keep it warm, a dolphin has a thick layer of fat under its skin. This special fat is called blubber.

These bottle-nosed dolphins show off their sleek, smooth bodies as they leap from the water. MARINELAND OF FLORIDA

Dolphins can swim very fast. Spotted and Pacific white-sided dolphins have been clocked at 23 miles (37 kilometers) per hour. The Dall's porpoise is also a speedy swimmer, but no one has timed it yet.

Pacific white-sided dolphins. DAVID AMBROSE, NATIONAL MARINE MAMMAL LABORATORY

How Dolphins Swim

When a dolphin swims, it looks very different from a fish. The fish moves its tail from side to side, but the dolphin tail goes up and down. The two halves of the tail are called flukes. The flukes have no bones in them. They are powered by strong, thick muscles in the dolphin's body.

Tail flukes. DARRYL W. BUSH/
MARINE WORLD AFRICA USA

13

Dolphins have a pair of flippers near the front of the body. The flippers help a dolphin steer its body through the water. When it swims slowly, it sometimes moves the flippers up and down. Most river dolphins have especially large flippers.

It is hard to believe that the flippers are like our arms. But if you look at a dolphin skeleton, you can see the finger bones inside the flipper. The skeleton will also show that dolphins have a few bones left from the hind legs. These bones are deep inside the body.

Almost all dolphins have a dorsal fin along the back. The dorsal fin helps balance the body as it speeds through the water. Most river dolphins have only a ridge along the back instead of a real fin.

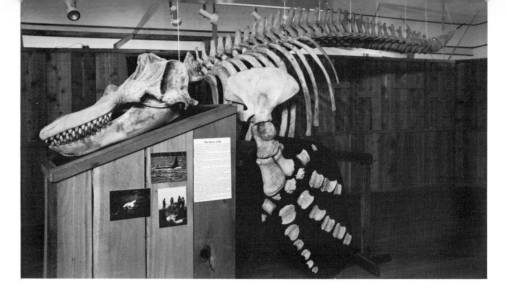

You can see the finger bones in the flipper of this killer-whale skeleton.
© KEN BALCOMB

The killer whale has a big dorsal fin. FRED FELLEMAN/THE WHALE MUSEUM

14

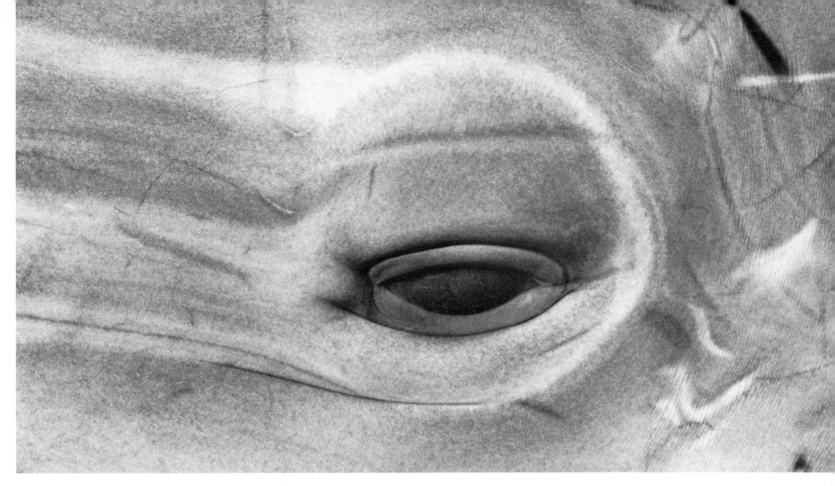

A dolphin eye. DARRYL W. BUSH/MARINE WORLD AFRICA USA

Five Senses

A dolphin's senses are not like ours in some important ways. After all, being surrounded by water is very different from living in the air. Dolphins' eyes are on the sides of their bodies. They can't see straight ahead like we can. But they can see quite well both in the water and out of it.

The streamlined dolphin body has no outside ears that stick out. The ear openings are just small holes behind the eyes. But the dolphin's ears are very special. Some of the noises dolphins make are ultrasonic, too high for us to hear. But the dolphins can hear them. Dolphins make fast clicking noises as they swim. When the clicks echo back from objects in the water, the dolphins can tell what obstacles are ahead. This special "sonar" is very sensitive. Dolphins can locate an item as small as a BB with it.

Besides their clicks, dolphins also make whistles, squeaks, barks, and yapping sounds. These are used to communicate with other dolphins. Unfortunately, humans have yet to figure out dolphin languages.

Dolphins don't have a sense of smell. But recently, scientists discovered that dolphins do have a sense of taste. Like humans, bottle-nosed dolphins can detect sweet, sour, bitter, and salty tastes.

Touch is an important sense to dolphins. They often brush bodies or touch one another with their flippers.

Dolphins often touch one another as they swim. DAVID SCHMID, MARINELAND OF FLORIDA

The pilot whale can dive at least 2,000 feet (610 meters). STEPHEN MULLANE

Down in the Depths

When they are swimming near the water's surface, dolphins breathe more than once a minute. But they can hold their breath when they dive deeply.

The dolphin's body has special ways of helping it get oxygen during a dive. When the animal breathes before diving, almost all the air in its lungs is replaced by fresh air. That way, it carries as much oxygen as possible. The blood and muscles can also hold extra oxygen.

Mysteries of Stranding

Dolphins sometimes strand themselves on beaches. When people try to get them to go back into the water, they refuse to go. They just lie on the sand until they die. False killer whales and pilot whales commonly strand. Once, 835 pilot whales came up onto the same beach and died. Bottle-nosed dolphins, Atlantic white-sided dolphins, and other kinds strand, too.

No one understands why some dolphins behave this way. Some scientists think most of the animals are healthy but are following a sick leader that gets confused. When a single animal strands, perhaps it is ill. In shallow water, it can breathe without using energy to swim to the surface. Other scientists believe that dolphins use the magnetic field of the earth to help them find their way. Some places where dolphins often strand have an abnormal magnetic field. This might confuse the animals into coming ashore.

3

Social Life

Few dolphins live alone. Most spend their lives in groups called schools or pods, swimming and hunting together. Living in a group also makes it easier to find mates. The kinds of dolphins that stay along the coasts usually have small schools. Dolphins that live far out at sea, however, travel in huge schools of countless numbers. Perhaps this gives them protection against their enemies, the sharks.

Killer-whale pods are close family groups.
©KEN BALCOMB

Bottle-nosed dolphins. ©*STEPHEN J. KRASEMANN/DRK PHOTO*

Bottle-nosed Dolphins

The bottle-nosed dolphin is very familiar because it performs on television and at marine parks. These animals inhabit warm and cool seas around the world. There seem to be two kinds of bottle-nosed dolphins. One kind stays along coastlines. These animals live in small schools and even enter rivers for short periods of time. The school may consist of a large male and several females with their young. Or it may be made up of young animals that are not old enough yet to have their own families. Some schools consist only of adult males.

The schools aren't like family groups. Animals leave and join, so the group keeps changing in size and content.

The second type of bottle-nosed dolphin lives farther out at sea and around islands. Its schools are bigger, and have around twenty-five animals. These schools may join together to form even larger groups having hundreds of individuals.

Harbor Porpoises

The harbor porpoise is a small animal that lives close to the coast. A big harbor porpoise is 6 feet (1.8 meters) long and weighs around 200 pounds (90 kilograms). That makes it about the size of a large man. Sometimes, a harbor porpoise will swim up a river, but it spends most of its time in shallow seawater.

Harbor porpoises usually live in small groups of only two to ten animals. At times, however, they travel in herds of up to a hundred.

The Common Dolphin

The common dolphin inhabits all the world's oceans except near the poles. It is a beautiful, graceful animal that travels in huge herds. Out at sea, herds spanning over 30 miles (48 kilometers) and containing perhaps a quarter million individuals have been seen. The dolphins leap and splash, making the sea appear stormy and wild. These acrobatic animals can catch leaping fish in midair.

Other dolphins may join the common dolphin on its travels. Pacific white-sided dolphins and northern right whale dolphins are often found swimming with common dolphins.

Common dolphins. J. MICHAEL WILLIAMSON

23

Spinners and Spotters

The spotted dolphin and the spinner dolphin often travel together in large groups. They may be accompanied by schools of yellowfin tuna. The spotted dolphins and the tuna both feed on fish, squid, and crabs.

In modern times, the dolphins get into trouble by traveling with the tuna. They often get trapped in the nets of tuna fishermen. Since dolphins breathe air, they can drown if they can't reach the surface to breathe. Every year, thousands of dolphins die in tuna nets. In American waters, the government sets a limit on how many dolphins are allowed to die each year in this way.

Spinner dolphins get their name from their spectacular acrobatics. They jump straight up and spin around, nose to the sky. They leap from the water and tumble end over end.

A spotted dolphin leaping from the water. © STEVEN MORELLO

A spinner dolphin jumping. C. ALLAN MORGAN

4
Having a Family

Dolphin babies, like those of other mammals, grow inside their mothers' bodies. After being born, they feed on their mothers' milk, the way puppies and calves do. But living in the water creates special problems for dolphin babies.

Born Ready

The mother dolphin gives birth to one baby, usually nine months to a year after mating. Twins are very rarely born.

The dolphin calf must get to the water's surface to breathe

Killer whale mother and baby.

within minutes of birth. Sometimes, the mother dolphin nudges its baby upward for the first breath. But after that, it is on its own.

The baby stays close to its mother as it swims along. Since dolphins spend their lives on the move, the babies have to be strong swimmers from the moment they are born. They must keep up with the adult dolphins.

Dolphins are born especially large. A newborn dolphin is often half as long as its mother. Besides being able to swim well, it can hear and see right away.

A young bottle-nosed dolphin with its mother.
DAN FEICHT, CEDAR POINT, SANDUSKY, OHIO

Getting Fed

Drinking milk underwater is tricky. At first, the mother dolphin lies on her side so the baby can breathe while it nurses. Later it can hold its breath while it feeds.

The mother has two nipples hidden inside grooves along her belly. When the calf wants to nurse, it nudges its mother. A nipple pops out. The calf wraps its tongue around the nipple, and milk squirts into its mouth. It nurses only for a short time, but it feeds often. A young bottle-nosed dolphin will nurse about once every fifteen minutes.

A baby dolphin grows very fast. During the first year, it can double its length and become seven times as heavy. The rich milk it drinks makes such fast growth possible. Dolphin milk contains 40 to 50 percent fat, while cow's milk is less than 4 percent fat.

Caring for Babies

Although it grows fast, the dolphin calf needs care for at least a year. It may start eating some fish by the time it is six months old, but it continues to nurse for a year or more.

Other dolphins may help take care of the baby. One of them instead of the mother sometimes helps it get its first breath. When danger threatens, adults other than the mother may protect the young.

Panama, a bottle-nosed dolphin at Marine World Africa USA in Vallejo, California, nurses from her mother, Circe. DENNIS HADA/MARINE WORLD AFRICA USA

Bottle-nosed Babies

The bottle-nosed dolphin is the best-known to scientists. Bottle-nosed calves are born at different times of the year. In Florida waters, February to May is the birth season. Near Europe, they are born during the summer. Birth takes place a year after mating.

The new baby is 3 or 4 feet (1 to 1.25 meters) long and weighs 20 to 26.5 pounds (9 to 12 kilograms). For a year to eighteen months, it will drink milk from its mother. Female bottle-nosed dolphins are ready to bear young when they are about five years old. From then on, they will give birth every two or three years. Males don't breed until they are nine.

A bottle-nosed mother and calf.
MARINELAND OF FLORIDA

5

Feasting on Fish

Dolphins' favorite foods are fish and squid, animals that live in large schools. When a group of dolphins is hunting, it spreads out across the water. That way, the animals are more likely to find a school of prey. They also may peek out of the water, looking for feeding seabirds.

Finding Food

Dolphins have several ways of finding food. When the water is clear, they can use their eyes. A harbor porpoise, for example, may grab mackerel from the outer edges of a school, locating them by sight. Dolphins can also find fish by hearing the sounds they make.

In cloudy or deep, dark water, dolphins use their sensitive "sonar" to locate food. We can imagine that the dolphin is "seeing" with its ears. Scientists disagree on just how the sonar clicks are produced. Dolphins lack vocal chords. But a dolphin has a complex system of air channels and cavities in its head that is connected to the blowhole. Somehow, air circulating through these channels appears to produce the clicks.

White-sided dolphins herd a school of herring. Many of the fish are jumping out of the water. ©STEVEN MORELLO

The bump on the front of a dolphin's head, called the melon, may help focus the clicks into a narrow stream of sound. The melon is filled with oil that carries sound well. The skull under

The bottle-nosed dolphin has an obvious melon on the front of its head.
DAVID SCHMID, MARINELAND OF FLORIDA

the melon is dished so that it looks dented, which could also help focus the clicks.

Scientists aren't sure just how the echoes are carried to the ear. The jawbone may help. The sides of the melon may be involved in bringing sound to the ears, too.

Deep Feeding

Some dolphins dive deeply for their dinner. There is a layer of living things that feed on one another in the ocean. Countless tiny animals such as little shrimps move into deep water (as far as 3,000 feet, 900 meters) during the day and come closer to the surface at night. Squid and small fish like sardines feed on and move with them. At night, when this living layer is within 330 to 660 feet (100 to 200 meters) of the surface, dolphins like spinners dive down and eat the squid and small fish. Common dolphins also feed on them. Common dolphins can go down as far as 900 feet (280 meters) and stay under for eight minutes. During feeding time, the huge herds of common dolphins break up into smaller groups.

Helping Each Other Hunt

Groups of dolphins often help each other in chasing down prey. Bottle-nosed dolphins may form a line and chase a school of fish toward the shore. Then they feast on the fish in shallow water. They may also surround the school and trap the fish inside the circle.

Dolphins also chase schooling fish from below. The fish, trapped between the dolphins and the water's surface, ball up into a tight school. This makes it easy for the dolphins to grab mouthfuls of fish.

After a school of Pacific striped dolphins had encircled some fish, a scientist was able to reach in and pick up the fish by hand. The fish may have been exhausted from the chase. Or they could have been in a state of shock. But some scientists think that dolphins use their high-pitched sounds to stun fish. There is evidence that killer whales do this with herring, one of their favorite foods. And live fish put into tanks with captive dolphins sometimes become strangely paralyzed.

6
Dolphins and People

Bow Riders

Common and white-sided dolphins as well as spinners are experts at riding the bow wave of ships. The dolphin finds just the right spot, where the water pressure supports it. It spreads out its flippers and keeps its body still, moving right along with the boat the way a surfer rides a wave coming into a beach.

An individual dolphin may become hooked on bow riding. One dolphin, nicknamed Pelorus Jack, hitched rides with New Zealand ships for over twenty years.

A bottle-nosed dolphin leaps while riding the bow wave of an oil tanker. SUSAN H. SHANE

37

Friendly Dolphins

Most wild animals avoid contact with humans. But it is not unusual for healthy wild dolphins to associate with human divers. There are even stories of dolphins saving humans from drowning or guiding them to shore. Such stories may be exaggerated. But bottle-nosed and occasionally Atlantic spotted dolphins look like they enjoy swimming with people. Sometimes they even allow people to touch them. The dolphins may sport with the divers until the humans tire.

Wild dolphins come to play with children at Moneky Mia (Shark Bay) in western Australia. VINCENT SERVENTY

7
Dolphin Show-offs

Humans, because of their fascination with dolphins, have captured them and kept them in marine parks. Marineland of Florida was the first ocean park in the United States. It opened in 1938 and was also the first place to breed bottle-nosed dolphins in captivity. Since then, such parks have opened all over the country, often far from sea.

The killer whales Yaka and Vigga perform at Marine World Africa USA. DARRYL W. BUSH/ MARINE WORLD AFRICA USA

Putting on a Show

Dolphins are great entertainers. Their spectacular jumps and graceful leaps thrill audiences around the world. The most common performers are bottle-nosed dolphins. But pilot whales, killer whales, Pacific white-sided dolphins, and a few others have also been trained.

Dolphins in marine parks perform many tricks. They jump high in the air through hoops. They pull boats through the water. They fetch balls and balance them on their beaks. Often, a story accompanies dolphins' stunts.

Training Dolphins

Training dolphins is not difficult. They are willing to learn and catch on fast. Dolphins are usually trained with a whistle and a bucket of fish. If the trainer wants the dolphin to leap out of the water, he or she waits until the animal jumps on its own. The trainer blows the whistle and rewards the dolphin with a fish. Every time the animal jumps, the whistle blows and it gets a fish.

Trainer Jim Mullen works with a bottle-nosed dolphin at Marine World Africa USA.
DARRYL W. BUSH/MARINE WORLD AFRICA USA

Pretty soon, the dolphin is jumping over and over again, rushing up for a fish after each jump. Then the trainer must change the routine. The trainer doesn't blow the whistle and give the dolphin a fish until it jumps more than once. At first, the dolphin is confused. But soon, the animal realizes it won't get a fish with every jump. The next step is to blow the whistle only with high jumps. Soon, the dolphin knows it must jump higher to be rewarded. Once it understands that, it only gets fish with some jumps. Eventually, the dolphin learns to jump when it hears the whistle. In this way, the trainer uses the whistle and fish to let the dolphin know what is wanted. Bit by bit, a dazzling routine can be put together.

Trained dolphins seem to enjoy their work. After all, living in a concrete tank with blank walls must be boring. By performing, the animals get some attention and exercise, with fish thrown into the bargain.

8
Dolphin Intelligence

Dolphins seem smart in many ways. They are especially easy to train and understand quickly what their human trainers want from them. They live in groups and seem to care for one another. They have what sound like complicated languages. For all these reasons, many scientists have spent years studying dolphins to figure out how intelligent they are.

A group of dolphins jumps together at Cedar Point in Sandusky, Ohio. DAN FEICHT, CEDAR POINT, SANDUSKY, OHIO

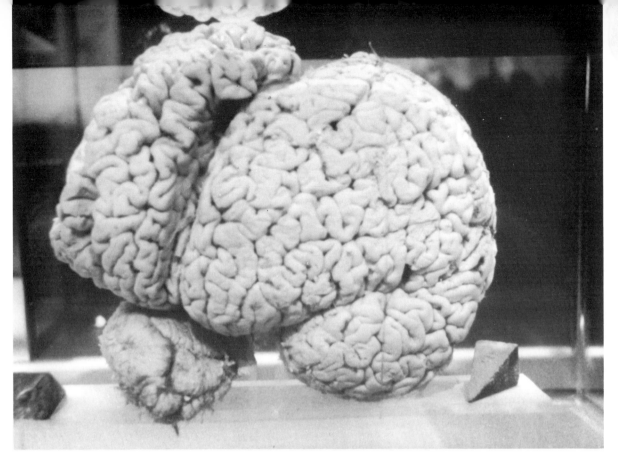

*The brain of a
Dall's porpoise.*
©ALISA SCHULMAN

Dolphin Brains and Human Brains

For their body size, dolphins have brains equal to those of humans. They have plenty of brainpower left after taking care of their bodies' needs. The brain of dolphins looks much like a human brain, too. The part involved with thinking is large, as in humans.

But the dolphin brain is put together differently from the human brain. Our brains have areas specialized for certain kinds of learning and thinking. But the dolphin's brain isn't like that. The different parts are very similar to each other.

Can Dolphins Understand Language?

Dolphins learn to follow commands easily. But can they understand language itself? Dr. Louis Herman wants to find out. For several years, he has been studying dolphin language learning. Dr. Herman and his co-workers have trained two dolphins. One, named Phoenix, has learned the meanings of underwater sounds made by a computer. One sound represents HOOP, a plastic hoop in the water. Another means FETCH—go pick up an object. Phoenix knows many words for objects like hoop and actions such as fetch. She also understands OVER, UNDER, THROUGH, LEFT AND RIGHT, SURFACE (of the water), and BOTTOM (of the tank). The different words she knows can be combined into sentences. With so many words, sentences she has never heard are made easily. The words are always given to Phoenix in a particular order.

The other dolphin, Akeakamai (ah-KAY-ah-kuh-my), Ake for short, knows a different language. Hers is a visual language. A trainer stands by the tank and uses arm signals for words. Each signal means a different word. Ake's language is different from Phoenix's in another way, too. The order of the "words" is not the same.

Trainers Carolyn McKinnie and Mark Hanson greeting Akeakamai (left)
and Phoenix (right) prior to beginning training of the dolphins.
© LOUIS M. HERMAN, KEWALO BASIN MARINE MAMMAL LABORATORY

Each dolphin learned her language well. When a totally new sentence was given, both usually performed correctly. For example, when Ake was signaled FRISBEE FETCH SURFBOARD, she brought the Frisbee to the surfboard. In her language, that was the correct response. SURFBOARD FETCH FRISBEE meant to bring the surfboard to the Frisbee. She could understand the difference between those two sentences.

Akeakamai correctly follows directions by carrying a hoop to a pipe.
ALAN LEVENSON, KEWALO BASIN MARINE MAMMAL LABORATORY

How Smart Are Dolphins?

There are limits to knowing how smart any animal is. The world of the dolphin is very different from ours. We have trouble imagining what it is like to live as dolphins do. And we have no idea how much dolphins are "saying" to one another with their whistles, yaps, and squeaks.

It will be a long time before we really understand very much even about bottle-nosed dolphins. But meanwhile, we can still enjoy the willing performances and the graceful beauty of these bright, fascinating animals.

Index

(Italicized numbers indicate photos)

Akeakamai, 45–46, *47*
Amazon River dolphin, *9*, 10
Atlantic spotted dolphin, 38

blowhole, 4, *5*, 32
blubber, 10
bottle-nosed dolphin, *1*, *11*, 21,
    27, *29*, 30, *31*, *37*, *40*, *41*;
    language understanding by,
    45–46
bow riding, 37
brains, *44*

common dolphin, 23, 37

Dall's porpoise, 12
dolphins and porpoises, birth,
    26–27; calf, 26–30; diving, 19;
    ears, 16; evolution, 10; eyes, 15;
    feeding, 32–36; friendliness, 38;
    intelligence, 43–47; milk, 28;
    performing, 39–42; senses,
    15–16; size of, 7; skeleton, *14*;
    skin, 10; smell, 16; sounds, 16,
    32; swimming, 12; touch, 16;
    training, 41–42
dorsal fin, *14*

flukes, *13*

harbor porpoise, 8, 22, 32
Herman, Louis, 45

killer whale, 6, 7, *14*, *20*, *26*, *39*

marine parks, 39–42
melon, *34*–35

Pacific striped dolphin, 36
Pacific white-sided dolphin, *12*
Pelorus Jack, 37
Phoenix, 45–46
pilot whale, *6*, *18*
pod; *see* school
porpoises, 6

river dolphins, 9

school, 20
sonar, 16, 32–35
spinner dolphin, *8*, 24, *25*, 37
spotted dolphin, 24
stranding, 19

teeth, 6

whales, 6
white-sided dolphin, *33*, 37